AACA: Business & Technology

ACCA, Volume 1

M. Imran Ahsan

Published by M. Imran Ahsan, 2024.

AACA: BUSINESS & TECHNOLOGY

First edition. February 26, 2024.

ISBN: 979-8224743322

Written by M. Imran Ahsan.

Preface

Here is a comprehensive guide to the ACCA Business and Technology course; you will find all the information you need to succeed.

Is "Business Technology: Mastering ACCA's Business and Technology" anything that interests you?

Brief Synopsis: Take a close look at businesses to learn about their inner workings, key players, and environment. We eliminate any complexity and ensure you have no problem learning these fundamental notions by offering simple examples and clear explanations.

"Business Technology: Mastering ACCA's Business and Technology Subject" goes above and beyond what is often found in textbooks. You may use it to your advantage in your ACCA studies since it simplifies complex concepts, provides real-world examples, and offers practical strategies.

Preparation is critical to succeed in the ACCA Business and Technology course. "Business Technology: Mastering ACCA's Business and Technology Subject" is an essential resource for anybody seeking to acquire knowledge, understanding, and skill in this field. Rest assured, you are fully prepared to crush ACCA!

To all knowledge seekers and smart learners

Chapter 1: ORGANISATIONS AND THEIR ENVIRONMENT

To successfully accomplish a goal, a group must first be structured and organized. The organization might be a business, a non-profit, the government, or other institution. Organizations are defined by their structures, employment, and tasks. They are motivated by a sense of purpose, goals, and objectives. People in groups offer their skills and time to help the group succeed. Individuals must be able to coordinate and communicate with one another to function well as a team.

Organizations need things like money, technology, and people to work. They follow the rules and laws that are in place. Each group has its own culture and set of beliefs. They need to be able to deal with changes in the world. Groups of people work together to complete tasks, and they have a big effect on society, business, and government.

A business organization is a group of people who work together to give customers goods or services in exchange for money. It can be a business that is run to make money, like a company or a shop. Organizations in business have a set framework and clear goals they want to reach. To do their work, they need things like money, tools, and people to work for them. A business's main goal is to meet the needs and wants of its customers while also making money and getting a profit.

All groups can be split up into smaller parts called subsystems. For instance, a business has sections like manufacturing, sales and marketing, and accounts. It's possible to split each section into even smaller parts. For example, the bookkeeping department has several sub-departments, such as cash, accounts, payables, and ledgers.

Close system/ close organizations: The name "closed systems" comes from the fact that these systems don't talk to other systems. There isn't much to these methods, and they don't last long. If a business doesn't pay attention to new technologies, competition, and customer wants, it will have a hard time succeeding.

Open system/ Open organizations: "Open organizations" do affect their surroundings. They take in information from their surroundings and send it back out into the world. The ones that are useful and important in the real world are these open platforms.

Types of organizations

Commercial Organizations: Companies whose primary goal is to increase their financial wealth are known as commercial organisations. Different legal structures are available for them, such as partnerships, limited liability partnerships, sole proprietorships, and limited liability corporations. In the event of financial trouble and liquidation, owners are better protected by limited liability partnerships and limited businesses. The owners are shielded from personal responsibility and creditors may only seize the company's assets in such a scenario. But partners and sole proprietors are personally liable for all company obligations to an infinite extent.

Commercial organizations are typically classified into different sectors:

Primary vs secondary sector: Resource extraction and processing are at the heart of the primary sector.

In the secondary sector, production is the main emphasis.

Offering products and services is what the tertiary sector looks for.

In some instances, a quaternary sector is distinguished, which includes R&D businesses like pharmaceutical and information technology.

Non- Profit organizations: The not-for-profit sector is another category of organizations. Charities, including nonprofit medical centres, are an example of a not-for-profit organization. Their accounting system is based on revenue and expenses rather than profit and loss. In order to stay afloat, non-profits must ensure that their revenue is more than or equal to their expenditures.

Public sector organizations: Public sector organizations are owned by the government, either on a federal or state level. The military, healthcare, and school systems are all examples of organizations that fall within the umbrella of the public sector. The government may have a stake in other sectors of the economy, such as national airlines, in some countries. Even while nonprofits may have a business motive, but that's not always the case.

NGOs: NGOs, or non-governmental organizations, are groups that work on a global scale and are usually not for profit. This group includes a large number of United Nations agencies.

Cooperatives: All of the people who work for a cooperative own a piece of it. As an example, in order to sell their goods better, farmers may form cooperatives. In cooperatives, members work together to achieve a common goal—the pursuit of profits—while also sharing in the ownership of the business.

Organization structures

Different types of organizational structures can be categorized as follows:

Entrepreneurial

Functional

Divisional

Matrix

Boundary-less

Organizational structures can be classified into several categories, including entrepreneurial, functional, divisional, matrix, and boundary-less structures.

Entrepreneurial structure: The most basic kind of an entrepreneurial organization is a manager and an employee team. Typically, these firms are tiny and operated by families. As a result, they don't need distinct divisions. Many times, the same persons serve as both owners and managers. A **functional structure is** often adopted when a simple company grows. Sales and marketing, accounting, payments, receivables, and R&D are just a few examples of the functions that can benefit from their own dedicated department. This organizational setup may be very successful due to the fact that each department is free to concentrate on what it does best, which in turn reduces overhead costs.

The main tasks in an organization can be grouped into different functions:

- Ordering and purchasing: This involves buying materials and assets from suppliers.
- Manufacturing/production: Creating goods that customers want to buy.
- Direct service provision: Providing specialized services like legal, accounting, or consulting work.
- Sales and marketing: Finding and selling to customers.
- Distribution: Getting products to customers, often through outside companies.
- Administration: Handling office tasks and record-keeping.
- Research and development: Creating new products or ways of making things.
- Human resources: Hiring, training, and managing employees.
- Accounting and finance: Dealing with payments, invoices, and financial statements.
- Cash and working capital management: Managing money and making sure there's enough to pay bills and expenses.
- Treasury management: The treasury department is an essential aspect of every large company's financial management system. Capital needs, issuing more shares, getting loans from banks, and figuring out dividend payments are all key aspects that they evaluate. They are also concerned with reducing interest

rates and foreign currency risk. Another part is lowering the company's tax obligations, which has been a gripe for a few famous businesses.

As businesses expand, a clear delineation between shareholders as owners, a board of directors as decision-makers, and managers as implementers of board decisions becomes more apparent. This is called **divisional structure**. Separating a company into subsets according to goods or locations could be useful if it keeps growing. Because every department deals with unique production, markets, competition, and laws, this setup enables them to focus on what they do best.

Matrix systems are more sophisticated. Imagine a collective project. Assume Project A has a project team and manager. Team members do work for this boss. For instance, one project manager may handle money and another quality control. Someone may also manage project workers. In a matrix firm, each employee manages projects and functions.

Each worker in a matrix firm reports to two individuals. They report to the project manager and department heads. This approach may appear harsh to conventional managers, but it's the realities and expectations of workers. Managers collaborate better using the grid framework. If Project B is behind schedule, Project B and Quality Control managers may collaborate to speed up quality control. After selecting a repair, quality control may implement it.

A boundaryless organization can take different forms:

Virtual: Creating a separate company outside the main organization to seize temporary market opportunities.

Hollow: Outsourcing non-core operations like accounting, human resources, legal services, and manufacturing, allowing the company to focus on its core strengths, such as designing new products.

Modular: Ordering components from various internal and external providers and assembling them into a final product.

5. Mintzberg's structures

Mintzberg divides organizations into five. Strategic apex—top management or the Board of Directors—is the first phase. Second is the middle line, where intermediate managers convey orders down the organization. The third portion is the operational core, which comprises daily workers. Fourth are support personnel like accounting and IT. Techstructure creates and enforces standards and processes like quality control manuals and employee handbooks.

These sections of the organization vary in size and significance each organization. A tiny entrepreneurial company has a strategy apex, functioning core, and little middle line, support personnel, and technostructure. A major accounting or law firm's middle line is shorter, reflecting a tighter interaction between the partners at the top and the audit or legal staff. Support personnel is large, but the technostructure is tiny. Standardized processes are less appropriate in these organizations since they personalize solutions to specific customers.

In summary, organizations have five parts: strategic apex, middle line, operational core, support personnel, and technostructure. These sections differ per organization in size and significance. Due to client-specific solutions, professional organizations have a shorter middle line and smaller technostructure.

6. Levels

Organizations are often seen as having three levels tactical, operational, and strategic. These levels are called the "Anthony hierarchy". The board of directors and the top managers make up the strategic level, which is at the very top. As part of their main job, they may make plans for the next five years as part of the organization's long-term strategy. In order to follow this plan, the business needs to decide where it will be based and whether it will switch from making things to offering services.

At the very bottom is the operational level, which is where daily tasks are carried out. Most of the jobs on this level are short-term and can be finished in one day. Planning doesn't take long—usually just one or two weeks. At this level, people's main job is to carry out deals or keep track of them. This means they write bills, handle orders, and answer customer questions.

In the middle is the tactical level, which is made up of area heads. The managers are busy making sure the budget and goals for the year are met, so they only have a year to make plans. They are also in charge of daily jobs, but their main goal is to set up their area to fit the year's budget and goals.

7. Tall/narrow, wide/flat

Organizations can be categorized as either tall-narrow or wide-flat. In a tall-narrow structure, each manager or supervisor has a relatively small number of subordinates, indicating a "span of control". On the other hand, in a wide-flat structure, the span of control is much broader.

In a tall-narrow organization, there are many hierarchical layers, and due to the small number of subordinates, there is close supervision. This type of structure is often described as bureaucratic, formal, and focused on strict job descriptions and grades. In contrast, a wide-flat organization is more egalitarian, with less hierarchy and greater communication between top and bottom levels. There is less emphasis on strict job descriptions and more focus on teamwork and getting the job done.

Many organizations consciously switched from tall-narrow to wide-flat buildings in the 1990s via "delayering" or "flattening." Two key variables caused this transition. First, cheaper Far Eastern manufacturing countries put pressure on costs. Western companies have to simplify processes and remove middle-man jobs to compete. Second, rapid technical improvements and worldwide market shifts required quicker organization responses. Multiple layers and resistance to change made the tall-narrow construction hard to adapt; therefore, wide-flat structures were used for agility and flexibility.

It is important to note that the term "scalar chain" refers to the hierarchical chain of command within a company, from the top to the bottom.

8. Centralization / Decentralization

Organizational structure and power are different. Two organizations with the same form might have differing authority for different employee ranks. Centralization or decentralization determines organizational power distribution. Decentralization may be useful or harmful.

Many benefits come from decentralization. First, top managers may feel overloaded and unable to concentrate if all decisions must go via them. Second, decentralization speeds up decision-making by eliminating the need to convey requests up the hierarchy. Thirdly, it lets experts make choices, improving efficiency. Fourthly, decentralization makes workers who like heading their own departments happy. Finally, it identifies people with good decision-making skills for promotions.

Decentralization may lead to poor coordination and ineffective decision-making. Divisions may make choices that benefit themselves but hurt the company. The head office or board of directors may need to intervene to guarantee department cohesiveness.

Downsizing to cut costs, delayering to gain flexibility, outsourcing non-core operations to specialized firms, offshoring to take advantage of lower labor costs, and implementing shared services to consolidate operations are recent organizational structure trends.

9. Formal and Informal

Organizations are formal and informal. Organization procedures manuals, and performance reviews purposefully construct and record formal organization. A large part of the organization is informal, including personal goals, group conventions, preferences, rumors, and alliances. The informal organization may considerably affect how people behave and interact; thus management must understand and control it.

Management knows about informal organizations, but comprehending their dynamics is difficult. Personal goals, connections, and departures from official rules might affect the organization.

Chapter 2: AN ORGANISATION'S ENVIRONMENT

The PESTEL model studies how the macro-environment affects firms. It stands for Political, Economic, Social, Technological, Environmental, and Legal Factors. Political changes, economic swings, societal trends, technical breakthroughs, environmental concerns, and legal requirements all have the potential to have an impact on enterprises.

Porter's 5 Forces model analyzes industrial sectors and their attractiveness. It examines five forces: competition or rivalry, buyer pressure, supplier power, prospective entrants, and alternative goods. These dynamics drive an industry's profitability and influence methods such as pricing changes, buyer relationships, supplier management, entry obstacles, and technology adaptation.

Porter's value chain describes how a corporation creates money. It is made up of major activities (inbound logistics, operations, outbound logistics, marketing & sales, and service) and supporting activities (firm infrastructure, technological development, human resource management, and procurement). The firm generates value by providing more for consumers than the expenditures connected with these operations. This might involve providing competence, convenience, economies of scale, or other benefits that clients are prepared to pay for.

SWOT Analysis: The strengths, weaknesses, opportunities, and threats of a company are assessed using the SWOT Analysis. Strengths and weaknesses such as product portfolio, human resources, tangible and intangible assets and financial strength are considered internal factors. External factors are opportunities and threats like competition, new innovation, technology and new market opportunities provide opportunities as well as dangers. These external factors are not in control of the company but can affect its profitability or strategic position. Businesses should fix weaknesses to protect themselves and use strengths to seize opportunities. A healthy relationship between internal and external factors is essential for a business to survive and earn profit. In order to attain profitability and long-term success, these analyses help businesses comprehend their environments, industry dynamics, value generation, and strategic positioning.

Chapter 3: AN ORGANISATION'S

STAKEHOLDERS

Stakeholders are individuals or entities influenced by the organization. There are three types of stakeholders:

Internal stakeholders are the stakeholders inside the company. They include workers and supervisors.

Connected stakeholders: Suppliers, consumers, shareholders, and lenders are examples of external stakeholders who have a contract with the firm.

External stakeholders who do not have a contractual relationship with the firm. They include the government and may also include people who live near the factory.

Stakeholder analysis is crucial because their interests often clash. Shareholders want bigger profits, and workers want better pay. Customers expect more quality at a cheaper price, but stockholders want more profits. Managing these conflicts requires compromise and keeping most stakeholders pleased, even while certain stakeholders have the ability to disrupt the company, such as workers going on strike.

One critical connection is between shareholders and directors/ management. Shareholders own the firm but are not engaged in its daily operations. Directors and management serve as representatives for shareholders. However, conflicts of interest may arise when directors prioritize their personal gains above shareholder profits, such as granting themselves hefty bonuses or investing in hazardous initiatives. To remedy this, corporate governance standards have been implemented to guarantee that directors behave in the best interests of their shareholders.

Mendelow's matrix is a method for evaluating stakeholders. It evaluates the stakeholder's power and interest. Key actors are stakeholders with significant influence and interest, and management must keep them satisfied. Stakeholders with strong authority but little chance of action may demand less attention, but they must still be pleased. Those with little authority but a lot of interest should be kept in the loop since they have the potential to influence critical actors. Stakeholders with minimal power and interest may be mostly disregarded since they are unlikely to act.

To summarize, knowing stakeholders and their dynamics is critical for conflict management and organizational success. Mendelow's matrix offers a paradigm for prioritizing stakeholder interaction depending on their power and interest levels.

Chapter 4: ORGANISATIONAL CULTURE

Significance of organizational culture and related concepts: The cultural web is defined as a depiction of the cultural influences that exist inside a corporation. These impacts include organizational assumptions, myths and tales, symbols and titles, rituals and routines, power dynamics, control systems, and organizational structure.

Charles Handy's four categories of organizational culture: power culture, role culture, task culture, and person culture. Power culture is defined by the concentration of power in the hands of a single person or a small group of people. Role culture is a management structure in which various individuals play different roles. the task culture prioritizes getting the work done and completing the assignment, with less focus on job descriptions and hierarchy. Person culture is a somewhat uncommon style in which employees seek personal goals inside the firm.

Schein defined three layers of culture: artifacts, values, and underlying assumptions. Artifacts are the most obvious and tangible elements, such as appearance and behavior. The values go deeper and represent the organization's declared aims and ideas. Underlying assumptions are the most basic level, representing the organization's underlying beliefs and expectations.

Hofstede model: Power distance, individualism/collectivism, masculinity/femininity, uncertainty avoidance, and long-term orientation are the five aspects of organizational culture that are identified by the Hofstede model.

Chapter 5: CORPORATE GOVERNANCE AND ETHICAL CONSIDERATIONS

Corporate governance is the management and control of businesses, with a focus on the separation of ownership and control. Shareholders own the corporation, but they pick directors to oversee day-to-day operations. Directors serve as intermediaries for shareholders and should act in their best interests.

Shareholders have less financial information, and they have fewer meeting opportunities to discuss company matters; it is difficult for them to actively monitor the directors. In order to solve this problem, strict corporate governance guidelines are governed and established.

The OECD has established six corporate governance principles. These principles are based on protecting shareholder's rights, promoting the fair and open market for healthy competition, and ensuring timely disclosure of any material information.

Six corporate governance principles are highlighted by the Organization for Economic Cooperation and Development (OECD). These include protecting shareholder rights, promoting fair and open markets, and guaranteeing prompt disclosure of material information. The Financial Reporting Council (FRC) is responsible for creating the United Kingdom Corporate Governance Code. This code highlights the need of strong corporate governance for long-term success and provides examples of examples of best practices.

The concept of corporate social responsibility (CSR) has gained prominence in recent years, and some individuals are beginning to question whether or not companies should put the interests of their shareholders ahead of anything else. Those who advocate for corporate social responsibility (CSR) contend that in addition to meeting their legal requirements, businesses should also take into account the interests of other stakeholders, such as society, the environment, and workers. However, adopting CSR activities may lower corporate earnings, sparking arguments over the scope of social duties and their beneficiaries.

Ethics in business are important for a variety of reasons. Acting ethically decreases risks and expenses, since unethical activity may lead to legal penalties, compensation claims, and reputational harm. Ethical conduct attracts excellent workers, fosters goodwill, and boosts consumer trust and sales. Companies should aim to be ethical for reasonable business reasons.

Ethics, laws, and regulations provide as rules for corporate conduct. Ethics may be considered from two perspectives: consequentialism (doing the most good for the greatest number of people) or duty (based on absolute moral values). Ethical standards may be either relative or absolute, and both has advantages and disadvantages.

Managers face a variety of ethical challenges, such as balancing profit and public good in industries like pharmaceuticals, ensuring health and safety without over testing in sectors like aircraft manufacturing, promoting equal opportunities in recruitment, and making ethical payments without engaging in extortion, bribery, or corruption.

Overall, corporate governance, CSR, and ethical conduct are essential for organizations to function responsibly, build trust, and achieve long-term success.

Chapter 6: SOME LEGAL OBLIGATIONS

Sources of Law: In the study of law, we explore where laws come from. In the European Union, European Union law prevails above national law. This might occur via regulations or directives. Regulations apply instantly to all member states, while directives require national governments to implement comparable legislation within a certain time frame. Case law is another source of law, especially in the United States and the United Kingdom, where higher court rulings serve as precedents for lower courts to follow.

Data Protection Act: Many countries have laws to safeguard personal data from abuse. In the European Union, this is accomplished via the General Data Protection Regulation (GDPR), which is applied in the United Kingdom under the Data Protection Act 2018. The legislation pertains to personal data of persons and establishes standards such as fairness, legitimate processing, accuracy, and security. Individuals have rights over personal data, including access, correction, erasure, and objection. Special requirements apply to data kept by the police and security services, and data transfers beyond the European Economic Area are prohibited unless individual rights are secured.

Risks associated with data include human mistake, technological issues, natural disasters, malicious hacking, industrial espionage, and dishonesty/fraud. Organizations must secure their data since loss or theft may result in financial loss, reputational harm, and possibly legal implications.

Health and Safety - Employer Responsibilities:

Employers are responsible under health and safety regulations. They must provide a safe and healthy work environment, maintain equipment to the required standard, provide information, instructions, training, and supervision to ensure safe practices, develop a safety policy, conduct risk assessments, share hazard information, identify at-risk employees, hire competent safety advisors, and form safety committees to address health and safety issues.

Health and Safety - Employee Responsibilities

Employees also have responsibilities for health and safety. Worker safety includes avoiding endangering oneself or others, not tampering with machinery or safety measures on purpose or carelessly, reporting potential dangers to the employer, and operating equipment correctly while using all available safety features.

Health and Safety Policy: Organizations have to draft and disseminate a health and safety policy covering general principles, protocols for dealing with particular hazards (like fires or toxic chemicals), legal requirements, specific guidelines for operating machinery, and necessary training for employees.

Chapter 7: ACCOUNTANCY, ACCOUNTS AND AUDITORS

There are a lot of different areas in accounting, such as:

Financial Accounting is responsible for defining accounting standards and regulating the manner in which information should be recorded in financial statements.

Auditing: Audits are required to be performed on companies as they grow in order to ensure that their financial statements accurately and fairly portray the company's current state of affairs. The auditors are the ones who perform auditing. They collect information impartially for the purpose of providing a report on the correctness of financial accounts.

Government: Accountants also work in government sectors. They usually monitor and report government funds like taxes and government expenditures on different developmental and non-developmental projects.

Management Accounting: Management accounting is different from financial accounting, and it is maintained for the purpose of higher management to review their performance, make budgets, and predict future revenues. They are maintained in a way that helps in making better decisions.

Taxation: Accountants also help businesses to calculate and submit taxes to the govt and govt entities.

Consultancy: Accountants also work as a consultant. They can provide consultancy services on company matters like informational technology systems and internal controls.

Accountants are professionals who demonstrate qualities such as competence, honesty, integrity, reliability, flexibility, respect for others, and self-control.

Professional ethical standards are developed by organizations such as the International Federation of Accountants (IFAC). These codes define duties for acting in the public interest and provide advice on basic concepts and ethics. Accountants must identify and handle compliance concerns, implementing controls to eliminate or mitigate them.

The Association of Chartered Certified Accountants (ACCA) has its own code of ethics and conduct. Its guiding values are integrity, objectiveness, professional competence and due care, confidentiality, and professional conduct.

Accounting information is used by managers, shareholders, trade contacts, financiers, tax authorities, employees, financial analysts, advisors, government agencies, and the general public.

Accounting data is separated into management and financial accounts. Management accounts are internal, customizable in style, primarily concerned with budgeting and performance monitoring, and are not subject to audit. Financial accounts, on the other hand, are published accounts that meet regulatory requirements, contain historical financial data, and are auditable.

Independent auditors undertake external audits to guarantee that a company's financial statements are accurate and fair. They study financial statements, evaluate internal controls, and provide management reports. Auditors do not , generate financial accounts, guarantee their accuracy, seek for fraud, or provide investment advice.

The regulatory system for financial statements in the United Kingdom includes company law, accounting standards, auditing standards, and ethical standards established by organizations such as the Financial Reporting Council (FRC), International Accounting Standards Board (IASB), International Federation of Accountants (IFAC), and International Ethical Standards Board for Accountants (IESBA).

These organizations provide rules and norms for financial reporting, auditing processes, and ethical behavior in the accounting field.

Chapter 8: INTERNAL CONTROL, FRAUD

Internal controls are processes used by businesses to guarantee that transactions are properly approved and documented, and that assets are protected. Businesses must have a strong internal control system as part of their corporate governance responsibilities. Directors and managers are responsible for ensuring the proper implementation of an internal control system.

Internal controls may be separated into two components: the control environment and detailed control procedures. The control environment is the organizational culture around internal controls. Some firms value having a strong internal control system, while others may see it as a hindrance. To be successful, the internal control system must have a strong control environment in which people value and follow internal controls.

Detailed control methods include particular measures that provide appropriate control over numerous parts of the firm. For example, when a person works overtime, their supervisor should approve it. Once a supplier's invoice has been paid, it should be canceled to avoid repeating payments. Before providing items to a new consumer, seek credit references and establish a credit limit. Delivering items over a customer's credit limit should be forbidden. Reviewing receivables and following up on late payments may help avoid bad debts. Another significant control mechanism is segregation of responsibilities, which involves having separate people handle distinct aspects of a transaction to limit the possibility of fraud and mistakes.

Internal control methods include physical safeguarding of assets like cash and inventory, authorization processes such as approving overtime, segregation of duties to distribute transaction responsibilities, reconciliations to compare financial records, trial balances and control account reconciliations, recalculation and re-performance of transactions to ensure accuracy, internal audits, and maintaining separate client bank accounts for businesses that deal with clients.

IT systems provide distinct dangers to internal control and information systems. Errors in IT systems may swiftly interrupt several transactions, resulting in operational disruptions, lost revenue, higher expenses, wrong judgments, and reputational harm. IT system risks include inaccurate data processing, unauthorized access to data, risks associated with multiple users accessing a common database, excessive access privileges for IT personnel, unauthorized changes to data and systems, failure to update systems in line with legal and business requirements, potential loss of data or restricted data access due to factors like viruses, hacking, or disasters, and cyber-attacks by external actors seeking to change or steal.

Controls in computer systems may be divided into two types: general and application controls. **General controls** are rules and procedures that apply to the whole computer environment and facilitate the operation of application controls. They comprise controls for data center and network operations, system software acquisition and maintenance, application system acquisition and maintenance, access security, and internet-connected system protection.

Application controls are human or automated procedures at the business process level that guarantee transactions are allowed, correct, and complete when recorded, processed, or reported. Application controls include edit checks for input data, numerical sequence checks, drop-down menus to limit selections, batch total checks, and online real-time transaction tracking.

Companies that do not have substantial internal control and corporate governance may suffer a lot from **fraudulent activities** and, consequently, pay penalties. They have to pay financial penalties for fraudulent activities leading to financial losses. Due to fraudulent activities, the employees tend to misrepresent the company`s assets and financial position which can damage the firm's reputation. Fraudulent activities usually happen due to several factors, including motive, incentive, opportunity, and lack of internal control, as well as lack of ethical training.

To detect and prevent fraud, the company needs to have a strong internal control system and establish strong ethical values in the whole organization. The employees should be given proper training to avoid being intentionally and unintentionally involved in fraudulent activity. Some activities that can reduce the chances of fraud are an internal audit system, proper authorization of payments, and reconciliations are necessary. The employees must be given on-the-job training about the latest fraud trends.

Money laundering is the process in which criminals convert illegal money into other assets that seem to be legitimate to show it as legally earned money. Money laundering involves three stages or steps: placement, layering, and integration. Placement means placing illegal money into the financial system by cash deposits or purchasing high-value assets. Layering means transacting the money in a complicated manner in order to hide the trail and to make it impossible to trace back the original source of that money. At last, as a final step, integration in which the money is introduced into the regular economy as "clean" money.

Money laundering is a big problem globally, and regulatory bodies all over the world seem to be at war with it through different forms of laws and regulations. Different methods have been used to detect and prevent money laundering to finance illegal activities. Financial institutions must adopt the Know Your Customer (KYC) process to verify and monitor their clients regularly. If they find any suspicious activity, they must report it to the concerned authority in their business jurisdiction.

Chapter 9: BUSINESS USE OF COMPUTERS AND IT

Spreadsheets: Spreadsheets like Microsoft Excel are mostly famous and are vastly known. They are composed of columns and rows making cells. They are used to contain text and numbers and to perform different mathematical and logical formulae. The spreadsheets used are usually used for making budgets, cash flow projections, and visual presentations, charts and graphs are made in these sheets.

Databases: Datasheets, which are more complicated than spreadsheets, may carry a large quantity of data and be shared across several departments within a firm. These databases are constructed by regularly employing linked files. These databases can perform a variety of complex operations and may be queried using SQL (structured query Language) to get specific data.

Big data: Big data is used for enormous volumes of data that are collected to discover trends and patterns. Big data has three distinguished characteristics, namely, volume, diversity, and velocity. Volume means a very vast amount of data; diversity means different types of data are collected. Velocity means a continual collection and processing of the data. Big data is used by many industries, including banks, consumer retail companies, educational and entertainment providers, and even by governments. To store this data cloud storage (offsite storage) and onsite storage like where houses are used. Different analytical techniques are used on this data, like cluster analysis, data mining, time series analysis, etc.

Artificial intelligence (AI): Those technologies that make it possible for machines to have intelligence are referred to as artificial intelligence (AI). It encompasses methods such as machine learning, picture recognition, voice recognition, and deep learning. AI can automate processes, improve decision-making, and mimic human intellect. Auditing, fraud detection, predictive modeling, and other fields may all benefit from AI. It allows machines to learn, recognize patterns, and forecast based on data analysis.

Accounting packages are software designed to manage company accounting. They verify that debits and credits balance and provide reports such as profit and loss statements, balance sheets, and dated receivables assessments. Accounting programs provide benefits such as speedier and more accurate record-keeping, faster analysis, and lower expenses. They are increasingly widely utilized, even by small enterprises.

Cloud computing stores and processes data on distant servers, rather than individual client devices. Users interact with the program via web-based interfaces and do activities on the server. Cloud computing increases flexibility, lowers hardware and software costs, and enables resource scalability. However, it demands continual internet access.

Blockchain technology creates a chain of records (blocks) that cannot be updated without discovery. This is known as distributed ledgers. Each block includes a hash of the preceding block, which ensures data integrity. The data is dispersed across numerous computers, resulting in a distributed ledger. This ensures the blockchain's security and resistance to assaults. Cryptocurrencies such as Bitcoin and Ethereum use blockchain technology to record transactions and ownership.

Chapter 10: MANAGEMENT

The word "management" has many acceptable definitions, the most common of which are: "Getting things done through other people." What this means is that management requires organizing and coordinating the duties of others. It highlights the importance of internal structure.

"A social arrangement where collective goals are achieved in a controlled manner." This management approach is on working with people and developing goals that everyone tries to achieve. Control is a very crucial aspect of management.

Supervision is both giving comprehensive instructions and keeping track on how effectively employees do their duties. Supervisors ensure that employees fulfill their duties, while managers make decisions and set targets.

Managers are often responsible for administrative tasks, particularly at the highest levels. It is the obligation of people under them to follow their valid directions, since they have authority owing to their managerial position. Managers pay great attention to current tactics and processes in order to do tasks effectively.

In contrast, **leaders** emphasize doing the right thing. Their primary emphasis is on the company's long-term goals and objectives. Motivating and influencing people is more vital than holding a high position in motivating others to follow a leader.

An Early management concept known as "**trait theory**." Its declared purpose was to uncover the attributes that good managers possess, such as intelligence, initiative, and self-confidence. However, the results were inaccurate, and the methodology was subjective. For example, finding a balance between appeal and intelligence was difficult. Being a good leader has nothing to do with an individual's measurement. Trait theory proved completely ineffective at predicting future managers.

Management based on Henri Fayol's theoretical foundation

Henri Fayol, an early twentieth-century management theorist, believed that management principles could be developed and taught. Managers, he said, should be able to plan, organize, command, coordinate, and supervise. However, Fayol overlooked the interpersonal aspects of management, as well as the need of inspiring and motivating employees, in favor of focusing on these responsibilities. It is not clear that splitting management tasks into several categories would result in greater success for managers.

According to Fayol's "classical management," an ideal form of administration exists that is founded on the same principles as classical architecture's focus on proportion. However, in its basic form, this concept is no longer popular.

Taylor Science-Based Administration

American thinker Frederick Taylor proposed scientific management in the late nineteenth and early twentieth century. He believed that labor should be researched and supervised thoroughly. Taylor emphasized the need of scientifically analyzing work in order to produce successful job designs, which lead to increased productivity and higher wages for employees. He argued that scientifically based methods should take precedence over rule-of-thumb ones. Taylor's ideas also influenced task specialization, which is typical in assembly line production today. Taylor drew criticism for allegedly humiliating labor, although his genuine purpose was to improve people' working conditions by increasing productivity.

Human Relations Institute

Elton Mayo conducted important experiments at the Hawthorne plant in the 1930s to investigate the influence of social factors on output. Mayo discovered that workers were more engaged and productive when they were involved in decision-making and made to feel valued. This resulted in the formation of the "human relations school," which contends that good management requires more than simply carrying out duties and must also consider interpersonal dynamics at work.

According to Mayo's study, informal groups at work have a substantial influence on employee behavior, and group norms play an important part in this.

Fashion Theories

Style theories suggest that management effectiveness is intimately tied to the manager's attitude to the work. However, whether these approaches help managers improve is debatable.

Peter Drucker suggested three functions for managers: directing the organization, managing other managers, and controlling personnel and their tasks. He categorized these tasks into five subcategories: objective formulation, group structure, motivation and communication, performance assessment, and people development. Drucker believes that in order for employees to reach their full potential, they must be driven and provided chances for personal development.

Mintzberg's Roles of Managers

Mintzberg identifies three sorts of managerial responsibilities: interpersonal, information processing, and decision-making. Interpersonal positions include formal authority, supporting information, and decision-making. Information processors are responsible for both data delivery and monitoring. A decisional role's tasks include making significant decisions and dealing with interruptions or conflicts.

Chapter 11: LEADERSHIP

According to the Ashridge Management College model, four distinct leadership styles exist. There is a continuum between these styles and various management philosophies.

The first is the absolute authoritarian approach, sometimes called "tells." Without offering any justifications, the boss merely gives orders to the personnel in this method.

A second, more convincing approach is known as "sells." In addition to giving orders, a good manager would also try to persuade their subordinates or explain why specific actions are necessary.

This brings us to our third style: "consults." Here, the manager consults with employees but then makes a call. It encourages active participation.

Type four is "joins" or "joins with." The manager may hold team votes or other forms of team participation in decision-making under this method. However, some believe this approach would make managers less effective in their guiding and regulating duties.

Blake and Mouton's managerial grid measures two aspects of leadership: concern for people and concern for the task. Managers may use the grid to assess their methods and find places to grow.

Managers who put their employees' happiness ahead of their own productivity are exhibiting the "country club" approach.

The command-and-control or task-oriented approach is rather than caring for their employees; these managers are laser-focused on getting things done.

The ideal kind of leadership is called "team leadership." An emphasis on both people and getting things done characterizes this approach. These managers know how to get things done while still caring about and meeting the needs of their employees.

Managers with a "middle of the road" approach, who care somewhat about people and tasks, are shown in the center of the grid. On the other hand, you want to go to the top right.

No one-size-fits-all method of management exists, according to contingent theories. Several criteria determine the most suitable style, including the people being managed, the task's urgency, and the resources that are accessible. It is crucial to be familiar with the significant ideas and writers linked with each theory of contingency since various theories provide light on different scenarios.

Considering the needs of people, the work at hand, and the team as a whole is central to Adair's action-centered leadership style.

The particulars of the situation dictate the best course of action. At times, it's more important to concentrate on getting things done quickly, but at other times, it may be necessary to resolve group conflicts or meet specific demands.

According to Bennis leaders and managers are two different things. Leaders think about the future, innovate, and build trust, whereas managers are more concerned with the company's here and now-and day-to-day running. Honesty, perseverance, generosity, modesty, transparency, and originality are some of the traits of effective leaders.

A number of concepts involving adaptive leadership were proposed by Heifetz:

Changing viewpoints between the "balcony" and the "battlefield" as needed.

Recognizing adaptive problems that need mental shifts rather than simple fixes.

Making sure those in charge of making changes are supported by a secure environment.

Considering the viewpoints and interests of leadership at different levels within the hierarchy.

Managing pain while offering solace and support.

Work in a logical sequence and set reasonable goals to avoid burning people out.

Maintaining concentration, handling disagreements well, and paying close attention to concerns are all examples of this approach.

Leadership style and favorable circumstances are the two variables that, according to Fiedler's thesis, determine how successful a leader is. Personal traits of the leader, especially their level of psychological distance from followers (cold vs. warm), are what make up their leadership style. The extent to which a leader is able to exert control and influence is relevant to the situation's favorableness. The best way to lead is conditional on how things are going.

According to Kotter Leadership, it is separate from management.

Chapter 12: Theories of Motivation

Motivation is the desire to go after one's objectives rather than idly contemplating them. In order to motivate their employees to work hard and accomplish company goals, managers must have a firm grasp of what drives people. Theories of motivation may be broadly classified into two groups: content theories and process theories.

Motivating work-related content or incentives is the primary goal of content theories. In contrast, process theories try to pin down the thought processes that lead to specific actions and the attainment of certain objectives.

Maslow's Hierarchy of Needs: According to Maslow's theory of needs, there is a human hierarchy of needs. He showed that there are five levels of human needs called hierarchies. These are physiological needs, safety, love and belonging, esteem, and self-actualization. The physiological needs for food, water, and shelter come at the bottom and need to be fulfilled first. After that, there comes the need for safety and security, which may include employment, health, and family. When these two needs are fulfilled, human look up for higher needs like love and belongingness. The fourth level is self-esteem, in which humans seek achievements, self-worth, and accomplishment. Last and final, human need in this hierarchy is self-actualization comprising morality, self-fulfillment, and realization of oneself. At this level, one searches for the pleasure and purpose of life. This theory can be used by companies for the betterment of their employees.

Although this theory is helpful, it's not without its drawbacks. The needs and preferences of humans can be different in different geographical locations and cultures. There may be more needs than Maslow has described.

Herzberg's hygiene theory: Herzberg's hygiene theory, or two factors theory, explains that there are two factors that motivate employees at work (or simply motivate any human being). One is motivators which increase the work happiness and hygiene factor prevent or reduce job dissatisfaction. Motivators include workplace satisfaction recognition and personal growth. Hygiene factors include extrinsic needs like remuneration, fair treatment, and relationship with the boss. Both of these are essential for the motivation of the employees.

The impact of valence and expectation on motivation is investigated in **Vroom's expectancy theory**, a process theory. A desired outcome is referred to as valence, and the possibility of attaining that outcome is evaluated by expectation. When you multiply valence and expectation, you get the motivating force. Offering desired objectives and a fair possibility of success are crucial for maximizing motivation.

McGregor offers Theories X and Y related to management styles and motivation . Theory X assumes that employees dislike work and need strict supervision, while Theory Y suggests that individuals view work as natural and seek social rewards and personal growth. A manager's ability to inspire their team members is contingent on his or her familiarity with the workforce and the methods used for leading it.

Motivation can be driven by **intrinsic and extrinsic rewards**. A feeling of accomplishment, challenge, and personal satisfaction are the sources of intrinsic rewards, while monetary compensation, public acclaim, and other forms of acknowledgment are examples of extrinsic benefits.

There are **two common ways to boost motivation**. First, involvement, which entails caring for workers, asking for their thoughts, and including them in making decisions. Second, job design, which may include job expansion (a greater diversity of duties), job rotation (a practice of transferring people to other positions), or job enrichment (a process of giving employees more responsibility and challenging work).

Using **money as an incentive** is not a simple task. It was eventually realized that it had motivational potential, although Herzberg first saw it as a hygiene aspect. However, there are obstacles to establishing a direct correlation between compensation and performance when issues like cost, salary ranges, and the difficulty of conducting fair and objective assessments of work performance come into play.

Several ideas have contributed to the complexity of the idea of motivation. An organization's ability to motivate its employees may be enhanced by taking the time to learn about each worker's unique requirements, implementing effective management strategies, communicating clear goals, and designing interesting work environments.

Chapter 13: Understanding Groups

In management philosophy, groups are crucial in their formal and informal forms. There are several distinguishing features of groups, including shared goals or objectives, strong group identification, established behavioral standards, and open lines of communication.

There are two main types of groups: formal and informal. The difference between formal and informal groups is that management consciously creates the former while the latter develops organically. On the other hand, good management requires familiarity with both kinds of groups. Elton Mayo's human relations management school was the first to recognize informal groupings, as shown in the Hawthorne plant research.

A formal group is formed when people with different backgrounds and expertise work together in a structured setting, like a team, they boost productivity. Team members may have expertise in manufacturing, accounting, and information technology, among other areas, while installing a new IT system. Chairperson, shaper, monitor/evaluator, business worker, resource-investigator, team worker, plant, completer/finisher, and specialist are some of the jobs that Dr. Meredith Belbin identified depending on psychological and technical characteristics. While it is great for teams to have a good mix of these responsibilities, it's crucial to avoid disagreements among them.

Tuckman's phases of team development provide valuable perspectives on how a group develops. The phases of formation, storming, norming, performance, and dorming are universal to all teams. During the forming stage, the group tentatively forms, but during the storming stage, members compete for positions inside the group. The performance stage occurs when the group efficiently operates and generates output after the norming stage, which specifies acceptable conduct and processes. The last stage of dorming is when the group gathers routinely without a tangible goal, which means it has to break up.

One of the most important things you can do to get effective output is to speed up the transition from forming to performing. One way to do this is to manage the changes in group composition such that disruptions are minimized.

Groups that are formally organized might be either teams or committees. With a clear goal in mind, team members pool their expertise and work under the direction of an assigned captain. However, committees are primarily concerned with making decisions; they bring together people from many departments to deliberate and reach a consensus. A committee's chair acts more as a coordinator than a leader, and the group's decisions are documented in writing.

When a team works well together, they have common goals, everyone pitches in, listens carefully, positively resolves conflicts, makes decisions based on consensus, delegating tasks clearly, regularly evaluating and improving their performance, and finally, they learn from their mistakes and adapt their methods to be even more effective in the future. The team leader is vital in creating an efficient team because they are responsible for establishing objectives, creating agendas, defining responsibilities, promoting equitable participation, helping to reach a consensus, defending minority opinions, and keeping track of and following up on action items.

A group's ability to communicate with one another may be emphasized via team-building activities.

Chapter 14: Recruitment and Selection Process

Because human resources are already limited and will only worsen, recruitment and selection play an increasingly important role in management. Reasons for this include the growing technological complexity of work and falling birth rates worldwide. The transition from manufacturing to service professions, including greater client engagement, makes finding the appropriate personnel even more challenging. As a result, businesses must specify their staffing needs and make an educated guess as to how many individuals they will need. They can advertise or work with recruitment agencies to attract potential candidates. In order to choose the best candidate, it is necessary to do a job analysis, write detailed job descriptions, and draft a person specification. BADPIGS is Roger's 7-point selection process that involves looking at a candidate's history, accomplishments, personality, physical characteristics, interests, IQ, and aptitudes.

To attract qualified applicants, it is necessary to provide a thorough description of the position while advertising open positions. Companies should not be too ambiguous in their requirements, since this can lead to inappropriate applications, but they should also include enough information to entice the proper people. Newspapers, websites, and job agencies are all good places to post ads. Interviews, reference checks, work samples, and group selection are some of the selection processes that may be utilized to delve further into applicants once applications have been received. A typical approach, interviews may be unreliable if not done by qualified interviewers in a well-structured environment. To have a deeper understanding of applicants, it is best to ask them open-ended questions and to offer instances of their talents.

Psychometric, proficiency, IQ, and aptitude tests are all part of the selection process that helps evaluate potential employees. Many

European nations have passed laws protecting people against discrimination in the workplace because of their age, gender, color, religion, handicap, or sexual orientation. Organizations must adhere to anti-discrimination regulations to guarantee equal treatment in employment, advancement, and pay. Indirect discrimination is when criteria inadvertently benefit one group over another, while blatant discrimination is when certain groups are purposely excluded. Retaliation against those who report prejudice is known as victimization.

Chapter 15: How People Learn

The Learning Process:

There are two approaches to learning theory.

a) The behaviorist approach: This view holds that punishment and reward play a significant role in our learning process. We are hardwired to do what gets us rewarded and stay away from what gets us penalized. Just because we react in certain ways doesn't suggest we know what we're doing.b) The cognitive approach: Understanding is the central objective of this technique. It maintains that our brains process sensory data by using logic and reasoning. Using this method, we look for patterns in our actions and the world around us. With the cognitive method, we can think our way out of any problem, giving us more leeway to adapt to novel circumstances.

Honey and Mumford:

Honey and Mumford identified four learning styles:

Theorists: To them, it's more important to grasp the theory before putting it into practice. Before doing anything new, they like to study the handbook or instruction book.

Reflectors: They pay close attention and think things through. Learning slowly and independently is their style.

Activists: They are opposite of theorists. Rather than plan ahead, they want to go right into things and discover the world.

Pragmatists: They are motivated when they see tangible advantages. Learning that helps them do their jobs better or easier is their main emphasis. Theoretical learning may be too much for them.

It is crucial to be aware of these different learning styles while instructing a group of individuals. It is preferable to provide a range of activities and techniques to cater to diverse learning preferences, as not everyone learns in the same manner.

Kolb - Experiential Learning:

Kolb postulated a model of learning in which there are repeated cycles of doing, reflecting on, and applying what we've learned. For instance, in the event that our presentation does not result in a contract, we analyze what went wrong and formulate hypotheses to improve our future presentations. We continue the cycle of learning from experience by using these ideas in the following presentation.

Development and Training:

Depending on the nature of the position, employees may get training in areas such as software or system usage. In contrast, development is more broad in scope and aims to equip people for future duties. Presentation, report writing, and interviewing abilities are common components of management training.

Good preparation is necessary for any kind of learning. The time and money spent on trainers, as well as the possible consequences of insufficient expertise, may add up to a hefty price tag for training. Training techniques (e.g., courses, coaching, self-study), budgets, and evaluations are all part of the planning process. Next is an analysis of workers' present and prospective abilities and competencies.

Staff morale, output, efficiency, initiative, safety, customer service, regulatory compliance, and the ability to delegate and adapt tasks should all be improved via well-designed training programs.

Chapter 16: How an Individual Can Develop

Personal Development Plans:

Improving oneself may be done in two ways: formally and informally. Formally refers to attending courses and finishing assignments. Grooming throughout a job experience is one example of an informal approach to improvement. The goal of grooming may be to improve performance in the present position as well as to prepare for future careers.

It is essential to prioritize the acquisition of transferrable abilities to guarantee optimal personal growth. Whether it's being an expert Excel user or a confident public speaker, these abilities are adaptable and useful in many settings. Possessing transferable talents makes one more marketable to potential employers and opens doors to new job opportunities. Pursuing careers that are a good fit with one's interests, beliefs, and ability to make a difference is an important part of personal development.

Learning new talents is essential for personal development. These in-demand talents, such as public speaking and adapting to new technology developments, increase an individual's value in the job market, opening up new professional prospects. While you have more options, choosing a profession that matches your personality, beliefs, and interests promotes personal growth.

Setting and working toward reasonable goals is also essential for personal development. To create appropriate objectives and prevent too broad goals, the SMATER framework technique is useful.

SMARTER" framework:

Specific: The goals must be specific. Instead of looking for overall progress, aim for specific goals like learning Spanish rather than learning a new language.

Measurable: Measurable milestones, such as standardized testing, should be considered when evaluating progress.

Agreed: For higher degree of dedication, one should buy-in courses and get encouragement from the mentors and other fellow learners.

Realistic: Always set reasonable goals to avoid demotivation.

Time-bound: Set a frequency for evaluating your progress, such as twice a year or regularly.

Review: Make sure the strategy is still relevant and effective by reviewing it on a regular basis and making any necessary revisions.

Competence/Competency Frameworks:

Competency frameworks outline the principles, knowledge, and abilities that are required for certain job functions. In order for staff development to reach its full potential, they provide clear direction and explanations. Typical components of a competency framework include an overarching definition of the competency and a set of observable traits, practices, and competencies that demonstrate mastery in that domain. To discourage unproductive actions that impede progress toward excellence, negative remarks may also be used.

Competency frameworks are useful for several reasons; they help in hiring, employee development, and product/service improvement. Furthermore, people may evaluate their own strengths and places for improvement with the use of these frameworks. The frameworks lay out the ground rules for the organization's culture, instill the right mindsets in employees, specify the responsibilities of managers, and advise potential hires of what to anticipate. They are a part of the hiring procedure and evaluation techniques.

Time Management:

Employers value employees who can effectively manage their time. It entails prioritizing work, creating a strategy to achieve the objectives, and using the SMART framework. Crucial is the ability to distinguish between significant and urgent tasks. Important things should be done, but not in a rush, whereas urgent things must be attended to immediately. Time is better allocated when priorities are established. An effective workflow is achieved by placing jobs logically and considering dependencies.

You need to learn how to manage your time well to avoid missing deadlines, wasting time, frustrating your coworkers, and alienating your customers. To avoid these problems, you must learn to manage your time well.

Coaching, Mentoring, and Counselling:

In today's corporate world, coaching, mentoring, and counselling are very beneficial activities.

Getting coaching means learning from more seasoned workers who can show you the ropes. As a result, it is often performed while on the job and offers valuable assistance with routine duties. As a client's proficiency grows, a coach may loosen off on their oversight as they continue to aid in the client's skill development.

One of the main goals of mentoring is to help mentees develop a lasting connection with an influential person who can encourage them and speak out for what they believe in. A mentor is like a trustworthy buddy on the job; they are there to help when you need it most and provide advice when things go tough. They provide a secure environment where employees may talk about anything, including conflicts with their bosses.

Individuals get non-directive advice via counselling. The goal of the organization is to make everyone feel more comfortable, boosting production and efficiency. Counsellors aid in the decision-making process by providing clients with a range of alternatives and guiding them in exploring their preferences.

Job happiness and organizational success are both enhanced by these activities, which contribute to personal and professional progress.

Chapter 17: Performance and Appraisal Interviews

Human resource management would be incomplete without performance evaluations. There are two primary goals: enhancing corporate performance and personal development. The company and its workers should both gain from this process.

Inspiring people to grow is the goal of performance evaluation. In accordance with Maslow's hierarchy of wants, it helps workers feel appreciated while also assisting them in developing their abilities.

Communicating with workers about their progress, areas for growth, and achievements is crucial to improving organizational performance. The company's total success is directly related to how well each person does their job.

There are typically three parts to an appraisal interview: compensation, an assessment of past performance, and predictions for the future. The incentive component goes beyond simple performance to consider market rates and affordability. Therefore, some experts recommend keeping it distinct from the other two.

It is critical to perform appraisals correctly. The evaluation is an opportunity for employees to get insight into their performance over the last year, and they frequently have to wait for it. Reviewing prior evaluations, work requirements, evaluations from peers and supervisors, and recognizing achievements are all part of the preparation process. Appraisals that are not well-executed risk being dismissed as meaningless formalities.

In order to conduct an effective appraisal, it is necessary to reduce obstacles such as personal enmity, prejudices, intimidation, and biased reporting. Managers need to be open to constructive criticism and take the time to identify problem areas. Instead of pointing fingers at workers, we should focus on helping them do a better job via direction and encouragement.

Multiple techniques may be used during the appraisal interview:

Tell and sell: To help the employees reflect on their performance, the manager gives them an evaluation form detailing their strengths and improvement areas. A manager's goal is to persuade an employee that their point of view is correct. This strategy is seen as useless.

Tell and listen: While expressing their own viewpoint, managers often invite employees to comment and give their own ideas. This method encourages open dialogue by giving workers a voice in solving issues, achieving goals, or expressing disagreement with evaluations.

Problem-solving: Ideally, the management and employee would examine the performance together and come to a mutual decision. In order to implement this strategy, thorough dialogue is essential.

Managers should ensure their employees are on the same page on future expectations, summarize the meeting, and provide a two-part report after the evaluation interview. The employee receives one copy, including the agreed-upon goals and outcomes, while the other is retained in the personnel file.

Essential follow-up tasks include arranging for necessary training and facilitating any agreements reached during the evaluation, such as a temporary transfer to another department.

Chapter 18: The Importance of Communication in Business

When it comes to corporate operations, communication is critical, particularly for tasks like control, coordination, and planning. The phases of the communication process are vital to comprehend, however, since they are more complicated than they first seem.

The stages involved in communication are as follows: concept formation, expression encoding, transmission (via sound, letters, or emails), reception, decoding, and feedback provision. Any of these points may cause communication to fail: a muddled idea, hazy encoding, interrupted transmission, an undelivered message, or inaccurate decoding.

Organizational communication may be horizontal (among coworkers in the same department), diagonal (between separate departments), or vertical (between superiors and subordinates). Official memos are an example of formal communication, whereas casual talks are an example of informal communication.

Information needed for communication differs at different organizational levels. Information gathered at the strategic level (upper management) is a mix of internal and external sources, often presented as significant numbers, and includes past and future projections and many guesses. The data stored at the operational level (transaction recorders) is routine, factual, historical, and highly accurate.

Miscommunication can arise from several sources; for example, when people use jargon or language that others do not understand when there are status differences between people at different levels of an organization, when people's emotions get in the way, when people use the wrong medium to transmit information, when people are reluctant to give or receive feedback, and when there is too much information to sort through, making it hard to prioritize messages.

Efficient and successful communication is brief yet thorough enough to be understood, relevant, timely, accurate, convincing, and cost-effective.

Leavitt classified many forms of communication: Y shape, wheel shape, circle, and chain. In a **Y-pattern** group, participants sit in separate groups and can only talk to the leader. This pattern is quite complex because three distinct groups are included within a single group. There is one leader who controls all three of these factions.

Wheel pattern: The captain of the team stands at the center of the wheel while the rest of the squad stands at the same level. Among the four patterns we looked at, this one was among the finest. This is the place where everyone can talk to the boss face-to-face. One drawback of this group is that members are unable to communicate with one another, and sometimes, even members of different levels are unaware of who is presenting at their level.

Groups organized in a **circle** pattern have a leader and follow a strict hierarchy. The group's leader may converse with the person who brings the net to their attention. The leader cannot communicate with the lowest-ranking members.

The hierarchical communication arrangement symbolized by the chain is known to be sluggish and restrictive. A building with a wheel form suggests rapid and focused communication with power concentrated at the center. In contrast to the Y-shaped representation, the circular form indicates slower communication.

For an organization to run well, its members must be able to communicate effectively.

Chapter 19: Macroeconomics

Introduction to Macroeconomics

Economics as a whole, including both domestic and global economies, is known as macroeconomics. Measurement of a country's economy, growth promotion, comprehension of unemployment rates and their causes, inflation management, currency exchange rate determination, and import/export analysis are some of the subjects covered.

Government Influence on Business

Businesses are greatly affected by the policies enacted by governments. Among these policies are economic ones that influence things like taxes, the cost of financing, and total demand. Tariffs and quotas are two examples of the many ways in which business regulations control market activity. Transportation and carbon emissions are two examples of environmental and infrastructural issues that need careful planning, budgeting, and efficiency. Education, pensions, and job security are all aspects of society that social programs aim to improve. Enforcement of export and import prohibitions, compliance with foreign trade rules, and membership in international trade organizations are all matters of foreign policy.

National Income

An indicator of a country's economic health is its national income. This number measures the overall worth of all newly created products and services in a given year. In order to prevent the practice of double counting, the national income is calculated exclusively using the sales revenue of the final sellers. More money is available to spend by the people of a country when the national income is high.

The Circular Flow of Income

Firms and households are interdependent, and the idea of a circular flow of income acknowledges this. For businesses to profit, households provide their labor, land, and capital in return for payment in the form

Chapter 20: Microeconomics

Introduction

Microeconomics is the study of decisions and resource allocation on a small scale, including at the individual, household, and business levels. Its most common context is markets for goods and services.

The demand curve

How much of a good people are willing to pay for is shown by the demand curve. In most cases, the amount requested falls as the price goes up. Several variables influence where and how steeply the demand curve is sloping, including product pricing, consumer income, availability of alternatives and complementary products, personal preference, and whether the product in question is a need or a luxury.

Price elasticity of demand

The price elasticity of demand measures the degree to which demand fluctuates in response to changes in price. When demand is elastic, it responds strongly to changes in price. A low degree of price elasticity of demand means that price changes have little impact on demand. A price elasticity of demand greater than 1 signifies elasticity, while a value between 0 and 1 denotes inelasticity.

Calculation of price elasticity of demand

When we compare the proportionate changes in demand and price, we get the price elasticity of demand. More precisely, it is "the percentage change in quantity demanded divided by percentage change in price. When determining elasticity along the demand curve, it is crucial to consider both the midpoint method and point elasticity.

Income elasticity of demand

Income elasticity of demand measures how demand changes with income. It is "the percentage change in quantity demanded divided by percentage change in consumer income. Positive income elasticity indicates normal goods, while negative income elasticity indicates inferior goods.

Demand and supply curves

The link between price and quantity desired is shown by demand curves, whereas the relationship between price and amount delivered is shown by supply curves. What we call "market equilibrium" happens when supply and demand are in harmony and the price is set.

Shifting the demand and supply curves

Several variables, including changes in income, the cost of alternatives or complements, expectations, consumer preferences, and population expansion, may cause shifts in the demand and supply curves. The equilibrium price and quantity are affected by these changes.

Cost curves

Fixed costs are those that remain constant regardless of output, whereas variable costs are those that rise as output does. While average variable costs first decline before rising again owing to diminishing returns, average fixed costs fall as production grows.

Types of competition

A perfect competition would include several small-scale, price-taking buyers and sellers. Oligopolies, monopolies, and monopolistic competition are all forms of imperfect competition. Strategic pricing and non-price competition characterize oligopolies and monopolistic competition, in contrast to monopolists' control over prices.

The main areas of study in microeconomics are product supply and demand, price, and the actions of buyers and sellers in different types of markets.

Chapter 21: Marketing

What is marketing?

Marketing entails finding a target market, satisfying their requirements, and then making a profit. It entails figuring out what people want, making it, and then giving it to them. Determining the size and profit potential of the market is also a part of marketing.

To understand marketing better, it's important to compare it with other approaches.

Product-led approach: Engineers and other creatives whose work places an emphasis on technical aspects and creativity are the primary targets of this strategy. Even if a product is well-designed, it could fail to sell because of high prices or a lack of demand.

Sales-led approach: The focus here is on making sales regardless of whether the buyers have a genuine need or desire for the advertised goods. Its reliance on convincing sales tactics raises the risk that buyers would come to regret their decision.

In contrast, the marketing-led concept looks outward and considers:

What potential customers want and appreciate.

The value they place on the product or service.

By conducting market research, marketers can understand customer needs and develop products or services that fulfill those needs. The focus is on customer satisfaction and building long-term relationships.

Market segmentation

It is important for marketers to know whether the market can be separated into groups or if all prospective consumers have the same tastes before they build goods or services. Factors like age, gender, lifestyle, income, and location are used to divide the market into smaller subsets called segments. The needs and tastes of various sectors could differ.

When it comes to the fashion industry, for instance, younger and older consumers have distinct tastes. One other factor that influences people's choice of clothing is their gender.

Additionally, one must take into account one's lifestyle, wealth, and disposable income. The majority of clothing lines include both economical and high-end alternatives.

By dividing the market into smaller, more manageable pieces, marketers may better meet the needs of their target demographics and increase sales.

Market targeting and the marketing mix

Market targeting follows market segmentation and entails deciding which segments to concentrate on. In order to appeal to a wider range of customers, many companies provide a variety of items. Marketers use the marketing mix, a set of interrelated tools, for effective marketing.

Seven Ps of marketing: The original "Four Ps" were product, pricing, promotion, and place. But today there are seven Ps in the extended marketing mix:

Product: Product attributes, design, quality, brand, and packaging all fall under this category.

Price: Pricing, sales, terms of payment, and strategic pricing are all part of it.

Promotion: Marketing strategies like as ads, promotions, direct sales, and PR are all part of this. Television, print publications, and the World Wide Web are just a few of the many mediums that may carry advertisements. Promotional sales include Combo sales and coupon sales. Public relations aims to increase positive coverage, whereas personal selling is crucial for business-to-business transactions.

Place: This relates to the product's accessibility in terms of both distribution and retail locations. The appropriateness of the outlet and the length of the distribution chain are factors to be considered.

Marketers use these factors to choose where to place their goods and services in the marketplace, which in turn increases demand and satisfaction among buyers.

Meeting consumer demands, achieving corporate objectives, and building successful customer connections are all possible when organizations grasp marketing ideas and use the marketing mix.

Don't miss out!

Visit the website below and you can sign up to receive emails whenever M. Imran Ahsan publishes a new book. There's no charge and no obligation.

https://books2read.com/r/B-A-ZWUK-ATAYC

BOOKS 2 READ

Connecting independent readers to independent writers.

Also by M. Imran Ahsan

ACCA
AACA: Business & Technology

CFA level 1
Corporate Finance for CFA level 1
Equity Investment for CFA level 1, 2020
CFA level 1 2020 Fixed Income
Economics for CFA level 1 in just one week

Investment series
Corporate Finance: A beginner's guide
Fixed Income Securities: A Beginner's Guide to Understand, Invest and
Evaluate Fixed Income Securities

About the Author

I am a PhD scholar and is a university lecturer for more than 11 years. I have been teaching Finance and Economics at various levels.

As an instructor I believe in simplicity, comprehensivity and in conciseness. I believe in smart kind of hard work. It means you should use your time efficiently to achieve optimal goals with limited time and efforts.